What Every
Must Know

Daniel Nana Kwame Opare

What Every Believer Must Know
Copyright © 2015 by **Daniel Nana Kwame Opare**. All rights reserved.

No part of this publication may be reproduced, stored in a retrieval system or transmitted in any way by any means, electronic, mechanical, photocopy, recording or otherwise, without the prior permission of the author except as provided by USA copyright law.

All characters appearing in this work are fictitious. Any resemblance to real persons, living or dead, is purely coincidental.

The opinions expressed by the author are not necessarily those of Revival Waves of Glory Books & Publishing.

Published by Revival Waves of Glory Books & Publishing
PO Box 596| Litchfield, Illinois 62056 USA
www.revivalwavesofgloryministries.com

Revival Waves of Glory Books & Publishing is committed to excellence in the publishing industry.

Book design copyright © 2015 by Revival Waves of Glory Books & Publishing. All rights reserved.

PREFACE

The main motive of this book is to draw believers' attention from false doctrines concerning Holy Spirit baptism, water baptism, salvation and prayer. This book will enable believers to know their identity and heritage as children of God. This book also talks about the personality of Jesus Christ, His baptism and the importance of His death.

This book will also enable believers to know some of the Bible prophecies concerning the events of the end time. The Bible says, "For lack of knowledge my people perish. This book contains light to direct you. Read it to be wiser.

All the quotations in this book are taken from King James Version, New International Version and Gideon International Version of the Bible.

DEDICATION

To: sister Efua and all my siblings.

ACKNOWLEDGMENTS

I thank Almighty God for granting me wisdom to write this book.

I also thank Apostle Eric Nii Aryee, Pastor P K Opoku, Pastor Fifii Abeka-Sam, Elder Richard Koffie, Elder Peter Mensah, Mr. G.Y. Ashong the director of Shepherd Printing Press, Mr. M.A. Larbi and Mr. E.O. Addo for their immense contributions towards the success of this book. May the Lord reward them according to His riches in Christ Jesus.

Author

Daniel N. K. Opare

E-mail:roselmaclean@yahoo.com

nagasnagasty@aol.com

Tel.: +233(0)20 / +233-26 9851768

CHAPTER 1

A. WHO IS JESUS?

The personality of Jesus Christ as to who he is has become a major controversy in the Christendom as a whole. Some see him as the son of God; some also see him as God himself.

Nevertheless, what does the Bible really say he is?

The Bible says in I Timothy 3:16 that, "God appeared in the form of human being (who was in the person of Jesus Christ). Some Bible translators who don't believe this have replaced the God there with He. And who is this He?

The truth is, the Spirit who appeared to Moses in the form of fire in the bush and said I am the God of Abraham, Isaac and Jacob, the same Spirit is called: the Angel of the Lord, (Exodus. 3:2, 14:14) the Spirit of God, the Glory of the Lord, (Exo.40:33-34, Ezek.3:12 - 10:4, 10, 45:2-7) I AM THAT I AM, the Arm of the Lord, (Isaiah 51:5, 40:10) the Word of God and the Power of God.

However, Isaiah 40:5 and 53:1 tell us that, it was the same Spirit who is called the above names that took human nature and came to dwell with human beings in the person of Jesus Christ. (John 1:1-15)

Furthermore, it is written, "He came to his own and his own received him not." (John 1: 11) The question is, who came to his own?

The Israelites know only Yahweh or Jehovah as their God and nobody else. So therefore, He came to His own means that, Yahweh or Jehovah, that eternal Spirit who appeared unto Moses in the bush, came unto his chosen nation, "Israel", through which he would make salvation available to all nations, families and tribes in human form in the person of Jesus Christ.

So therefore, the Spirit who said to Moses my name is I AM was the same Spirit that came to this world through Mary. So no wonder Jesus said to the Pharisees, "Before Abraham was I am." (John 5:58) Jesus Christ was that God who appeared to Moses in the bush.

B. WHY DID JESUS COME?

God created human beings in his own image and likeness to enjoy His fellowship and to have authority over everything on the earth. It is written, "And God said, Let us make man in our image, after our likeness: and let them have dominion over the fish of the sea, and over the fowl of the air, and over the cattle, and over all the earth, and over every creeping thing that creepeth on the earth. So God created man in his own image, in the image of God created he him; male and female created he them.

And God blessed them, and said unto them, Be fruitful, and multiply, and replenish the earth, and have dominion over the fish of the sea, and over the fowls of the air and over every living thing (both physical and spiritual) that moves upon the earth." (Genesis 1:26-28)

Notwithstanding, He commanded Adam and Eve the parents of all human beings to abstain from the fruit of the tree of knowledge of good and evil; else they will die. (Genesis 3:16-17)

But they disobeyed God and their disobedient brought enmity and separation between God and all human beings. It also brought human beings under the power of the devil. It is written, "Then the devil, taking Him up on a high mountain, showed Him all the kingdoms of the world in a moment of time. And the devil said to Him, "All this authority I will give you, and their glory; for this has been delivered to me." (Luke 4:5-6)

Nevertheless, due to the tender mercies of God towards human beings, He decided to reconcile us back to Himself; and to deliver us from the power of the devil through a sacrificial death of a righteous man. "It is written, "All we like sheep have gone astray; we have turned every one to his own way; and the Lord hath laid on him the iniquity of us all. He hath put him to grief: when thou shall make his soul an offering for sin." (Isaiah 53:6-10)

But no human being is qualified to be used for the atonement or the sacrifice since we are all descendants of disobedient Adam. (Romans 5:12) For this reason, God Himself took human nature in the person of Jesus Christ to atone for us in order to restore us back to our original position. So therefore, Jesus came purposely to atone for human beings.

C. WHY DID JESUS BAPTIZE?

John the Baptist baptized with the baptism of repentance for the remission of sins, (Mark 1:4) but Jesus did not sin, though He was tempted in all things, yet He did not sin nor did He inherit the Adam's sinful nature because He was not born by the will of man but of the Spirit of the Most High. (Luke 1:35, Hebrew 4:15)

Jesus was baptized by John purposely to be made the world's scapegoat. The scapegoat is a lamb chosen by God to transfer unto it the sins of the Israelites by the High Priest to take them away into the wilderness. (Leviticus 16:10, 20 - 22)

John the Baptist was sent from God (John 1:6) through the priesthood family; (Luke 1:5 - 13) made to be greater than all the high priests who had the divine right to transfer the sins of God's people unto the lamb. John baptized Jesus by transferring the depth of the sin of the world caused by Adam and Eve into Jesus' account to pay for it at an appointed time. It is written, "Behold, the lamb of God who takes away the sin of the world." (John 1:29)

Immediately Jesus came out of the water after the baptism, he was carried away into the wilderness by the Holy Spirit (Mark 1:9 - 13) as the scapegoat was accustomed to. So, Jesus was baptized to take upon Himself the depth of the sin of the world to pay for it at an appointed time.

D. WHAT IS THE ESSENCE OF THE DEATH OF JESUS CHRIST?

However, before the importance of the death of Jesus Christ, is elaborated, let's consider this vital question. If the Spirit who said to Moses, I AM the God of Abraham, Isaac and Jacob, was the one that took human nature and came to dwell with human beings in the person of Jesus Christ, then why did Jesus say My God! My God! Why have you abandoned me?

It is written, "The Holy Spirit will come upon you, and the power of the Highest will overshadow you; therefore, that Holy one who will be born will be called the son of God." (Luke 1:35)

According to the above scripture, Jesus Christ was both Divine and human. However, it was His human nature that was needed for the atonement.

Therefore, his Divine nature had to give way for the human nature to pay the penalty of the sin of the world caused by Adam and Eve.

For this reason, his Divine nature left him and his human nature which was needed for the atonement, felt the pain of the full penalty of the sin of the world and that caused him to say My God! My God! Why have you abandoned me? The God used here was His Divine nature who dwelt in him. (John 14:10)

Now, when the time for which Jesus came and also was baptized had fully come, he died to pay the full and perfect price of sin as required by God (Isaiah 53:3 -12) to reconcile the world back to God. (Colossians 1:20, Romans 5:10)

The Bible says that, "He who knew no sin was made sin for us, that we might become the righteousness of God in Him. Jesus died to pay the penalty of the sin of the world and resurrected again to show that, we have been justified". (1corinthians 15:14-22)

So because of the death of Jesus Christ, nobody is seen as an enemy before God in the world again, but salvation is for only those who accept Jesus Christ as Lord and Saviour and walk according to His will. It is written, "There is therefore no condemnation to those who are in Christ Jesus, who do not walk according to the flesh, but according to the Spirit." (Romans 8:1 KJV)

CHAPTER 2

A. WHAT DOES THE STATEMENT, EXCEPT A MAN BE BORN OF WATER AND THE SPIRIT, HE CANNOT ENTER THE KINGDOM OF GOD MEAN; AND WHY?

Jesus said unto Nichodemus, "Except a man be born of water and of the Spirit, he cannot enter into the kingdom of God".

This is because; water and the Spirit are the means by which a person becomes a new creature. It is written, "If any man be in Christ, he is a new creation.

Old things are passed away; behold, all things are become new". (2Corinthians 5:17)

God created human beings in His own image and likeness which simply means, to act morally and function as God. God made human beings perfect to enjoy His fellowship forever.

But when Adam and Eve, the parents of all human beings disobeyed God, and ate from the forbidden tree of knowledge of good and evil, they died spiritually; meaning, they were separated from God. They fell from their original state.

They lost their position of being the rulers of the earth to the devil. They became slaves to the devil. Hence, they were possessed by the spirit of sin also known as the law of sin.

Their inner beings which were made up of the characteristics of God such as love, goodness, kindness, etc., became dormant due to the possession and the indwelling of the spirit of sin which is also known as the law of sin; hence, man's inner being became sinful.

It is written, "The heart is deceitful above all things, and desperately wicked". (Jeremiah 9:17)

It is also written, "The imagination of man's heart is evil from his youth." (Genesis 8:21)

And this sinful inner nature of man also known as Adamic nature; was spread to all human beings since we are all descendants of Adam and Eve. (Romans 7:17-23, 5:12, Genesis 3: 20)

However, due to the tender mercies of God, He said in Ezekiel 36:26-27 that, I will give you a new heart and put a new spirit in you. I will remove from you your heart of stone and give you a new heart of flesh.

And I will put my Spirit (Holy Spirit) in you and move you to follow my decrees and keep my laws.

According to the above scripture, God made a promise to take away the Adam's sinful nature, the heart of stone also known as the law of sin that makes a person to be sinful, and replace it with the heart of flesh also known as the law of life or righteousness, as well as to endow us with His own Spirit, the Spirit of God (Holy Spirit) in order to be free from the power of sin.

And the water and the Spirit, which stands for acceptance of Jesus Christ as Lord and Saviour and water baptism are the processes by which God fulfills the above promise.

But Nicodemus, one of the members of the council, the governing body of the Jews, having believed in Jesus Christ in his heart, refused to confess him publicly for fear of dismissal from the council; therefore he secretly wants Jesus Christ to show that he believes in him.

But as it is written in Luke12:8 and Romans 10:10 that,

"Whoever confesses me before men, him will I also confess before the angels of God, for with the heart man believeth unto righteousness; and with the mouth confession is made unto salvation, believing in heart alone cannot save.

Therefore, Jesus drew his attention to the complete salvation processes by saying unto him; except a man be born of water and of the Spirit he cannot enter the kingdom of God.

The water and The Spirit, Jesus used here to represent water baptism and Jesus Christ himself respectively. It is written, "The Spirit is the Lord" (11Corinthins 3:17)

So therefore, the statement simply means that no one can enter the kingdom of God without receiving Jesus Christ as Lord and Saviour and water baptism. It is written, "He that believeth and is baptized shall be saved." (Mark 16:16, Act 2:38)

So water and the Spirit are the complete salvation processes as well as the new creation.

But this does not mean there is once saved forever saved, no. Works of righteousness follows it.

Note this complete salvation process do not require worked of righteousness; it is solely on the basis of grace: but after it, works of righteousness follow.

Now, the Water and the Spirit; When a person receives Jesus Christ as Lord and Savior, instantly, he or she receives forgiveness of sins, deliverance from spiritual death (separation from God) and the kingdom of darkness or the devil; but does not spiritually ushered into the kingdom of light, the family of God until the water baptism.

This is the reason why water baptism is an instant command. It doesn't demand any acceptance from the believer. It is an instant ceremony immediately after the acceptance of Jesus Christ as Lord and Saviour. (Mathew 28: 19, Acts 8:36-38, 10:47, 2:38-)

The Water baptism

Baptism is derived from a Greek word 'baptizo' meaning to be immersed or dip into.

When a person who has accepted Jesus Christ as Lord and Saviour is baptized, the seed of the devil known as the spirit or the law of sin which is also symbolized as the heart of stone, as well as every filthy, sinful and slavery attire or garment of the devil popularly known as Adamic nature, is removed and buried.

Then after, the believer is adorned with a new spiritual garment. He is also infused with the law of life, the seed or the spirit of righteousness which is also symbolized as the heart of flesh or the new man.

Afterwards, the believer is spiritually ushered into the household of God. It is written, "In him you were also circumcised, in putting off of the sinful nature, not with a circumcision done by the hands of men but with the circumcision done by Christ, having been buried with him in baptism and raised with him through faith in the power of God, who raised him from the dead." (Colossians 2:11 - 12,)

It is also written, "Know ye not, that so many of us as were baptized into Jesus Christ were baptized into his death? Therefore, we are buried with him by baptism into death: that like as Christ was raised up from the dead by the glory of the father, even so we also should walk in the newness of life, for he that is dead is free from sin; For as many of you as have been baptized unto Christ have put on Christ" (Romans 6:3-4, 7, Galatians 3:27)

So therefore, water baptism is the means by which the sinful nature of a person who has accepted Jesus Christ as Lord and Saviour is put off, as well as a spiritual initiation ceremony for ushering a believer spiritually into the household of God.

Hence, whoever has been born again is no more in the Adam's sinful nature as many believers do quote when praying for forgiveness of sins: "I am a descendant of Adam and I was born in sin."

When a person who has accepted Jesus Christ as Lord and Saviour is baptized, the features of God such as love, goodness, kindness, etc., which were possessed by the law of sin, are revived due to the in-plant of the spirit of righteousness, the law of life and the removal of the law of sin, the spiritual force which forces every human being to sin.

So, the 'expression,' "No one can enter the Kingdom of God without being born of water and the Spirit," simply means, no one can enter the Kingdom of God without receiving Jesus Christ as Lord and Saviour and the water baptism. (Mark 16:16)

Note this; even though God has set us free from the law and the power of sin through Jesus Christ, yet He did not touch our 'will'. We are still free moral agents. For this reason, be heavenly minded in order to overcome the desires of the flesh.

B. WHO IS A MEMBER OF THE CHURCH?

The Church or the body of Christ is made up of everyone who has accepted Jesus Christ as Lord and Saviour and has been baptized. It is written, "He that believeth and is baptized shall be saved." (Mark 16:16, Acts 2:38)

Water baptism, apart from being the means by which the sinful nature of a person who has accepted Jesus Christ as Lord and savior is put off, it is also the means by which a believer in Christ is initiated into the family of God, the church which is the body of Christ.

So therefore, every believer automatically becomes a member of the Church after baptism. It is written: "Now therefore, you are no longer strangers and foreigners, but fellow citizens with the saints and members of the household of God, having been built on the foundations of Apostles and prophets." (Ephesians 2:19-20)

The foundations of Apostles and prophets are: repentance, acceptance of Jesus Christ as Lord and Saviour, water and Holy Spirit baptism. (Acts 2:38)

But unfortunately, some Christians say that water baptism is not important because of the criminal who was saved on the cross without water baptism. (Luke 23:34)

But they have forgotten that, he repented at the point of death without the opportunity of water baptism. Even aside the above, he was also saved under the old covenant. The new convent which requires water baptism was established immediately after the death of Jesus Christ.

Is every member of the Church automatically entering Heaven?

No, having been a member of the Church does not mean every member will automatically enjoy eternal life, the life of total peace, joy and harmony with God as some Christians claim.

The doctrine of "once saved forever saved" is not true. The doctrine of once saved forever saved means to those believers that, every member of the Church or the body of Christ will automatically enter heaven irrespective of what he or she does since Jesus Christ has died for our sins.

But they have forgotten that, we have been called by grace into the Church or the body of Christ to justify our inclusion into the heavenly kingdom by submitting to the will of God. (2Timothy 4:18) It is written, "Many are called, but few are chosen." (Matthew 22:14)

The doctrine of once saved forever saved believers, base their doctrine on 1 Corinthians 3:13-15 which says that, "Every man's work shall be made manifest: for the day shall declare it, because it shall be revealed by fire, and the fire shall try every man's work of what sort it is. If any man's work abides which he hath built thereupon, he shall receive a reward.

If any man's work shall be burned, he shall suffer loss: but he himself shall be saved: yet so as by fire".

However, the above scripture has nothing to do with once saved forever saved; neither does it guarantee automatic salvation as they clam, no.

According to the above scripture, both rewards and salvation are by fire. "For if any man's work shall be burned, he shall suffer loss: but he himself shall be saved: yet so as by fire". This means that, salvation is also by works, works of righteousness. Hence it is written, "Know ye not that ye are the temple of God, and that the Spirit of God dwelleth in you?

If any man defiles the temple of God, him shall God destroy for the temple of God is holy." (1corinthians 3: 16-17)

Carnal minded Christians who walk according to the desire of the flesh such as formation, pride, etc., will not inherit eternal life, the life of total peace, joy and harmony, but spiritually minded Christians, who walk according to the will of the Spirit of God such as love, kindness, etc., will enjoy eternal life, the life of total peace, joy and harmony. (Romans 8:13-14, Galatians 5:19-22)

In fact, the Bible says in Hebrew 12:14 that, "No one can see God without righteousness." Righteousness is the only means a believer in Christ can enter heaven. It is written, "And, behold, I come quickly, and my reward is with me, to give to every man according as his work shall be.

Blessed are they that do his commandments, that they may have right to the tree of life, and may enter in through the gates into the city. For without (outside) are dogs, and sorcerers, and whoremongers, and murderers, and idolaters, and whosoever loveth and maketh a lie." (Rev. 22:12, 14, 15)

Jesus Christ has made us righteous by taking away the Adam's sinful nature, the old man, the seed of sin and has replaced it with the new man, the spirit of righteousness. It is written, "Do not lie to one another, since you have put off the old man with his deeds, and have put on the new man who is renewed in knowledge according to the image of Him who created him." (Colossians 3:9 -10)

So, whoever has accepted Jesus Christ as Lord and Saviour has been made righteous with everything he or she needs to overcome the sin.

Therefore, every believer who does not walk in this grace, but rather defile him or herself will not enter into the kingdom of God. It is written, "But the cowardly, unbelieving, abominable, sexually immoral, sorcerers, idolatries, and all liars, shall have their part in the lake which burns with fire and brimstone which is the second death." (Galatians 5:19 – 21, I Corinthians 6:9, Revelation 21:8, 27)

In fact, whoever has accepted Jesus Christ as Lord and Saviour has been delivered from the law of sin which forces every human being to sin and has been replaced with the law of life or the spirit of righteousness. It is written," For the good that I will to do, I do not; but the evil I will not to do, that I practice. Now if I do what I will not to do, it is no longer I who do it, but sin that dwells in me. For I delight in the law of God according to the inward man.

But I see another law in my members, warring against the law of my mind, and bringing me into captivity to the law of sin which is in my members. O wretched man that I am! Who will deliver me from this body of death? I thank God- through Jesus Christ our Lord! So then, with the mind I myself serve the law of God." (Romans 7:19-25)

Unfortunately, many believers in Christ use the above statement as a yardstick to indulge themselves in immoralities due to their lack of understanding of the statement.

The fact that the statement was rendered in the present statement form or simple present tense, does not mean, Paul the writer was still sinning after his conversion from Judaism to Christianity. When Paul became a believer in Christ, he never went back to his evil deeds which were as a result of the law of sin according to the statement.

So the statement, the good that I will do, I do not; but the evil I will not to do, that I practice, was a narration of his preconversion into Christianity evil deeds rendered in a present simple tense.

The whole statement was made to the Jews or the Israelites who accepted Jesus Christ as Lord and Saviour and yet still, practicing the Law of Moses.

According to the statement; every human being is possessed by the spirit or the law of sin.

But since God is righteous, and he wants every human being to be righteous, brought into the Law of Moses to compel every human being to be righteous.

But unfortunately, the laws of Moses, which was brought in to compel each and everyone to be righteous, did not do anything to deal with the law of sin which is the main cause of a persons immoralities; and for that matter the new covenant or the law of life through Jesus Christ was established to make us free from the law of sin which force every human being to sin.

So the statement simply means that every believer who has accepted Jesus Christ as Lord and Savior has been delivered from the law of sin which force every human being to sin which the Law of Moses could not deliver anyone from it. It is written, "There is therefore now no condemnation to them which are in Christ Jesus, who walk not after the flesh, but after the Spirit.

For the law of the Spirit of life in Christ Jesus hath made me free from the law of sin and death.

For what the law could not do, in that it was weak through the flesh, God sending his own Son in the likeness of sinful flesh, and for sin, condemned sin in the flesh: That the righteousness of the law might be fulfilled in us, who walk not after the flesh, but after the Spirit". (Romans 8:1-4) It is also written, "Knowing this, that our old man is crucified with him, that the body of sin might be destroyed, that henceforth we should not serve sin. For he that is dead is free from sin." (Romans 6:6-7, 18-17, 22)

For this reason, a believer has no excuse to continue to sin.

Jesus himself has made it clear to us in Matthew 22:12 that, whoever accepts him as Lord and Saviour is made righteous. He symbolized it with a wedding garment. According to Revelation 19:8, the garment is the righteous nature of the children of God.

However, since we have been made righteous by Jesus Christ free of charge, if we make our self dirty with sin we will be cast out into hell. It is written, "The son of man shall send forth his angels, and they shall gather out of his kingdom (Church) all things that offend, and them which do iniquity; and shall cast them into a furnace of fire but the righteous shall shine like the sun in the Kingdom of their Father." (Matthew13:41-43)

C. IS THE CHURCH A KINGDOM?

The Church or the body of Christ is a kingdom. Jesus said in John 5:27 that, "God has given Him authority to judge because he is the son of man."

The question is who is not a son of man? Whoever is born of man is a Son of man.

So why did Jesus say he has been given authority to judge because He is the son of man.

Jesus used this phrase, "The son of man" to refer to Himself as the Messiah who was coming to establish the kingdom. (Daniel 7:13 - 14)

But before he could establish the kingdom, he had to deal with the ruler of the world, popularly known as Satan as Jesus Himself admitted. (John 14:30). For this reason, Jesus said, "No one can plunder a strong man's goods without binding him first." (Matthew 12:29)

Now, how could Jesus bind Satan? When he was about to die, he said in John 12:31, that, "Now is the judgment of this world, now shall the ruler of this world be cast out." Casting out the devil does not mean he cannot operate again, but rather, to remove him from his position of being the ruler of the world.

Jesus cast out the evil on the cross by striking his head. (Genesis 3:15) It is written in Revelation 13:3; "And I saw one of his heads (powers) as if it had been mortally wounded and his deadly wound was healed."

He was wounded on the cross to reduce his powers until the Church is taken away (ruptured) before he will regain his total powers. It is written, "For the secret power of lawlessness is already at work: but the one who holds it back will continue to do so till he is taken out of way and then the lawless one will be revealed, whom the Lord Jesus will overthrow with the breath of his mouth and destroy by the splendor of his coming." (2 Thessalonians 2:7)

Moreover, not only the devil did Jesus disarm; he also disarmed all the powers of darkness. It is written, "Having disarmed principalities and powers, he made a public spectacle of them, triumphing over them in it." (Colossians 2:15) He disarmed them for the sake of the Church or the body of Christ. It is written, "I will build my Church and the gates of Hades (evil powers) cannot prevail against it." (Matthew16:18)

Literary, Hades means, the world of the dead; but based on the statement made by Jesus Christ, that, I will build my Church and the gates of Hades cannot prevail against it, the gates of Hades refer to the evil spirits.

It is the evil spirits or the demons that want the downfall of the Church and not the ghosts. It is written, "For we do not wrestle against flesh and blood, but against principalities, against powers, against rulers of the darkness of this world, against spiritual hosts in the heavenly places." (Ephesians 6:12)

Note, the evil spirits or the demons are also called the dead because they have been separated from God. Jesus disarmed the powers of darkness purposely for the sake of the establishment of the Church. It is written, "All authority in heaven and on earth has been given to me; Go therefore and make disciples of all nations." (Matthew 28:18-19, Revelation 1:18)

For this reason, the Church has been able to survive despite all the persecutions imposed on it by kings and Emperors backed by evil powers.

However, even though the Church or the body of Christ is made up of many people scattered all over the world, yet it is a kingdom whose king is Jesus Christ. It is written, "For he has rescued us from the dominion of darkness and brought us into the kingdom of the Son he loves." (Colossians 1:13)

It is also written, "You are a chosen people, a royal priesthood, a holy nation, a people belonging to God, that you may declare the praise of him who called you out of darkness into his wonderful light." (1 Peter 2:9, Hebrew 12:22-24, Revelation 1:5-6, 5:9-10)

CHAPTER 3

IS DEATH THE END?

Many people do say that, there is no life after death based on the statement made by king Solomon, that, "The dead know not anything, neither have they any more a reward; for the memory of them is forgotten their love, and their hatred, and their envy, is now perished; neither have they any more a portion forever in anything that is done under the sun" (Ecclesiastes 9:5-6)

In fact, the above statement does not mean when a person dies, he or she ceases to exist. All that the writer, King Solomon says here is that, when a person dies, he or she ceases to know anything that takes place on this earth; neither has he or she any share or portion of them.

In fact, life goes on after death. It is written, "And He was transfigured before them. His face shone like the sun, and His clothes became as white as the light. And behold, Moses and Elijah appeared to Him." (Matthew 17:2-3) If there is no life after death, where was Moses?

Jesus made it clear in his parable that, life goes on after death. In the parable, He said, Lazarus, the beggar; died and was taken into Abraham bosom and the wicked rich man also died and was taken to hell. (Luk16:19 - 20) If there is no life after death, then, why did Jesus make such statement?

In Exodus 3:6, God said to Moses, I am the God of Abraham, Isaac and Jacob without saying; I was the God of Abraham, Isaac and Jacob. God used the present tense "I am" instead of 'I was' too tell Moses that, Abraham, Isaac and Jacob still live.

Jesus confirmed this. When he was answering the Sadducees, the set of the Jews who does not believe the resurrection of the dead and the existence of spirits, He said unto them, "But concerning the resurrection of the dead, have you not read what was spoken to you by God, saying, I am the God of Abraham, Isaac and Jacob? God is not the God of the dead, but of the living." (Matthew 22:31-32)

In Isaiah 57:1-2, God said, "The righteous perish, and no one ponders it in his heart: devout men are taken away, and no one understands that the righteous are taken away to be spared from evil. Those who walk uprightly enter into peace; they find rest as they lie in death." If there is no life after death, then, why did God make such statement?

Life after death is real. It is written," When He opened the fifth seal; I saw under the altar the souls of those who had been slain for the word of God and for the testimony which they held.

And they cried with a loud voice, saying, "How long, O Lord, holy and true, until you judge and avenge our blood on those who dwell on the earth?"

Then a white robe was given to each of them; and it was said to them that they should rest a little while longer, until both the number of their fellow servants and their brethren, who would be killed as they were, was completed." (Revelation 6:9-11) If there is no life after death, then, why this statement?

The human being is made up of flesh and spirit. It is written, "It is sown a natural body, it is raised a spiritual body. There is a natural body, and there is a spiritual body. And so it is written, "The first man Adam became a living being" The last Adam became a life-giving spirit. However, the spiritual is not the first, but the natural, and afterward the spiritual. The first man was of the earth, made of dust; the second man is the Lord from heaven." (I Corinthians 15:44-47)

However, many believers call Jesus Christ the second Adam based on the above scripture. This scripture has nothing to do with Jesus Christ.

According to the above scripture, human being is made up of both flesh and spirit as written in Genesis 2:7.

The flesh comprises body and soul. The spirit dwells in the flesh. It does not die. When it leaves the flesh, physical death occurs. It is written, "When the spirit departs, they return to the ground." (psalm146: 4)

Where does the departed human spirit go?

The departed human spirit of the ungodly goes to a spiritual realm of no rest and peace known as Hell and the departed human spirit of godly goes to a spiritual realm of peace and rest called paradise. (Isaiah 57:2) Note; there is a difference between Hell and the Lake of fire: Paradise and Heaven.

Hell is a spiritual prison where the departed spirits of the ungodly human beings are kept until the judgment day. (1 Peter 3:19) And the Lake of fire is a spiritual realm of everlasting agony where the devil and his angels together with the ungodly human beings both those in Hell and the living will be cast into. (Matthew 25:41)

Paradise is a spiritual realm of peace and rest where the departed spirits of the godly human beings are kept until Jesus Christ appears. (1 Thessalonians 4:16) And Heaven is a place of everlasting harmony where the godly human beings, both those in Paradise and the living will be taken to. It is the city of God Himself.

However, on the judgment day, the departed human spirits of the ungodly, who are in hell together with the living who are ungodly as well as the devil and his angels will be cast into the lake of fire (Revelation 20: 15, Matthew 25:41) and the departed human spirits of the gods who are in Paradise together with the living who are godly will be taken to Heaven. (1 Thessalonians 4:16)

So, death is not the end of a person's life. Life continues after death. It is written, "It is appointed unto men to die but once, and after this the judgment." (Hebrew 9:27) For this reason, believe in Jesus Christ and walk in his ways, such as love, goodness, kindness and the like. It is the only way you can escape the eternal pain and suffering and enter into eternal harmony and joy; for there is no mercy for the unrighteous after death.

CHAPTER 4

IS A BELIEVER IN CHRIST UNDER THE MOSAIC COVENANT?

The Mosaic covenant is what is referred to as the old covenant or testament.

Many believers think that, we are still under the Mosaic covenant or the Law of Moses based on the statement made by Jesus Christ, that, "I have come not to destroy the law and the prophets; but to fulfill them." (Matthew 5:17)

In fact, to fulfill the law and the prophets does not mean they are not full; neither are they incomplete and he has come to make them full or complete as many believers do think. But rather, it simply means he has come to make them come to pass.

In fact, the Law and the prophets are about Jesus Christ. It is written, "And he said unto them, these are the words which I spake unto you, while I was yet with you, that all things must be fulfilled, which were written in the Law of Moses, and in the prophets, and in the Psalms, concerning me" (Luke 24:44)

And since it is about him, his life, words and deeds must not go against or contradict them, but rather, to make them come to pass… thus the statement, "I have come not to destroy the law and the prophets; but to fulfill them.

Now, on what basis was the old covenant or the Law of Moses established? It is written, "And God saw everything that he had made, and, behold, it was very good." (Genesis 1:31) If God saw everything that he had made and was very good, then, why did he say in Leviticus chapter 11 that, certain animals and fowls are unclean?

Again, God said, "Be fruitful and multiply." (Genesis 1:28) So, why then does God regard it as sin when a woman gives birth? It is written, "When a woman is conceived and gives birth, she is unclean: thirty days for a male child and sixty days for a female child. She should not touch anything holy or pertaining to God; neither should she enter the house of God. When the proposed days are over, she should bring a lamb for burnt offering and pigeon or turtledove for sin offering." (Leviticus 12:3-8)

Again, was it not God who made a man's semen to produce, why then did he say in Leviticus 15:18 that, if a man lies with a woman and has an emission of semen he is unclean?

Again, was it not God who made a woman's monthly cycle, why then did he say in Leviticus 15:19-24 that, when such thing occurs, the woman is unclean?

However, when God delivered the Israelites out of Egypt, He gave them Sabbaths to observe. He also commanded them to abstain from idol worship, but they disobeyed him.

And because of that, God's anger was kindled; and when his anger was kindled, he gave them the old covenant or the Law of Moses; hence, the old covenant or the Law of Moses was established out of God's anger. It is written, "Because they had not executed my judgments, but had despised my statutes, and had polluted my Sabbaths, and their eyes were after their fathers' idols. Wherefore, I gave them also statutes that were not good, and judgments whereby they should not live; and I polluted them in their own gifts, in that I might make them desolate, to the end that they might know that I am the Lord." (Ezekiel 20:24-26)

Now, what was the aim of the Sabbaths that they polluted? There are three main Sabbaths in the Bible. These are: the seventh Day Sabbath, the seventh year Sabbath and the Jubilee.

Each of these Sabbaths has its main purpose of establishment. None of them was instituted purposely as a period of worship. The main purpose of the seventh year Sabbath is found in Exodus 23:10-11 and that of the Jubilee is also found in Leviticus 25:8-13.

Now, the seventh Sabbath. The Sabbath was not instituted by God as a day of worship. Worship in those days was based on animal sacrifice: and it was every day business. One goat is sacrificed in the morning and one in the evening: and it was solely done by the priests on behalf of the whole nation. When the priests sacrifice the animals to God as worship, the whole nation has worshiped God. (Numbers 28:3-9)

However, on the Sabbath day, two additional animals were commanded by God to be sacrificed, and this serves as an offering for giving them a holiday.

Again, because they don't work on the Sabbath day, they were commanded by God to assemble themselves to hear the law from the priest in order to obey them: and this gave birth to the synagogues.

The synagogue assembly or worship which became popular in the days of Jesus Christ and the Apostles was not the main worship. The main worship was based on animal sacrifice, and it was solely done in the Temple or the Tabernacle: and it was every day.

So the Sabbath was not instituted as a day of worship, but rather, as a day of rest.

When the Israelites were slaves in Egypt, they never rested from working. The Egyptians, their masters never allowed them to rest even one day from working. They caused them to work everyday.

However, God, having known that the Israelites will make their slaves to suffer the same way, instituted the Sabbath to prevent them from causing their slaves and the animals they use to plow to work without rest as they went through Egypt.

It is written, "But the seventh day is the Sabbath of the Lord thy God: in it thou shall not do any work, thou, nor thy son, nor thy daughter, nor thy manservant, nor thy maidservant, nor thine ox, nor thine ass, nor any of thy stranger that is within thy gates, that thy manservant and thy maidservant may rest as well as thou.

And remember that thou were a servant in Egypt: therefore the Lord thy God commanded thee to keep the Sabbath." (Deuteronomy 5:14-15, Numbers 23:12)

Now, the Israelites, having broken the Sabbath and the various laws concerning righteousness and justice, God's anger was kindled and gave them the old covenant.

Nevertheless, due to the tender mercies of God, He promised to give them a new covenant. It is written, "Behold, the days come, saith the Lord, that I will make a new covenant with the house of Israel, and with the house of Judah:

Not according to the covenant that I made with their fathers in the day that I took them by the hand to bring them out of the land of Egypt; which my covenant they brake, although I was an husband unto them, saith the Lord." (Jeremiah 31:31-32, Hebrew 8:7-9)

This prophecy was fulfilled immediately after the death of Jesus Christ, the mediator of the new covenant and the old one, the Law of Moses with its regulations were ceased. It is written, "For verily I say unto you, Till heaven and earth pass, one jot or one title shall in no wise pass from the law." (Matthew 5:18)

This statement made by Jesus Christ, means that, the old covenant with its regulations will cease after His death. Immediately Jesus dies, and the veil in the Temple was toned, the old covenant or Law of Moses was closed and the new one was established. It is written, "Jesus Christ is the end of the law." (Romans 10:4)

It is also written, "Having canceled the written code, with its regulations, that was against us and that stood opposed to us; he took it away, nailing it to the cross." (Colossians 2:14)

So not only did Jesus die to reconcile us to God, he also took away the old covenant with its penalties and established the new one.

The new covenant constitutes faith in Jesus Christ, water and Holy Spirit baptism and righteousness.

Because of the death and resurrection of Jesus Christ, days, meats, circumcision, etc., have nothing to do with our salvation. We are to believe in Jesus Christ and walk in his footsteps which are: love, righteousness, kindness and the like. (Matthew 6:33) These are our license to heaven and not meats, days of worship, circumcision, Sabbaths and the like which have nothing to do with our salvation.

Even, if God has set a day to be worshiped, there cannot be any other day than the first day of the week because, everything first belongs to God. Example: God delivered the Israelites out of Egypt in a month called Abib. This month was not the first month of the year, but when God delivered them in this month, He made it the first month of the year. (Exodus 12: 1-2, 13:2,4)

Jesus Christ also resurrected on the first day of the week. (Mark 16:9)

Therefore, if there is a day of worship, there cannot be any other day than the first day of the week (Act 20:7, 1Corinthians 16:2) but days of worship, meats, circumcision and the like have nothing to do with our salvation.

It is written, "I know, and am persuaded by the Lord Jesus, that there is nothing unclean of itself: to him that esteemeth any thing to be unclean, to him it is unclean. For the kingdom of God is not meat and drink; but righteousness, and peace, and joy in the Holy Ghost.

For meat destroy not the work of God.

All things indeed are pure." (Romans 14:14, 17, 20)

It is also written, "Let no man therefore judge you in meat, or in drink, or in respect of a holiday, or of the new moon, or of the Sabbath days: which are a shadow of things to come; but the reality is of Christ." (Colossians 2:16-17).

Therefore, be conscience free in your Christian journey of Christianity is not a religion of bondage, but the life of God Himself...

CHAPTER 5

A. IS HOLY SPIRIT BAPTISM IMPORTANT?

There are three persons in the Godhead-the Father, the Son and the Holy Spirit. They form one indivisible God. (Matthew 28:19, 1 John 5:7 KJV)

The Holy Spirit is the third person in the Godhead. All divine equipment for God's work depends upon Him. (Acts 1:4-5, 8) The Holy Spirit baptism means, descending of the Holy Spirit to dwell in the believer: and it is important because:

1. He enables believers to understand the word of God. It is written, "When the Spirit of truth comes, he will teach you all things." (John 14:26) The disciples of Jesus did not understand His deeds and words until they were baptized by the Holy Spirit

When Jesus was about to be taken to heaven, His disciples said unto him; Lord, are you at this time going to restore the kingdom to Israel? (Acts 1:6) What kingdom were they talking about? They were talking about the restoration of the kingdom of Israel.

The Israelites were looking for the promise of God's Messiah who was to come from the house of David to deliver them from their enemies and the various empires they were under. (Micah 5:2-5, Jeremiah 23:5-6) Fortunately, the disciples recognized Jesus as the promised messiah. Because of this, they began to fight for the highest position in the kingdom since every king chose his officials to rule with them. (Mark 10:35 - 37)

For this reason, when Jesus declared to them that he was going to die, they became discouraged because of their expectation due to lack of understanding of the scriptures about what the kingdom they were expecting really mean; but when the Holy Spirit came on the Pentecost day, (Acts 2: 1 2) they understood the scriptures.

Example, Jesus said, "Baptize in the name of the Father, the Son and the Holy Spirit." (Matthew 28:19)

But the disciples baptized only in Jesus name. Why?

This is because, according to the above statement, there is one name of the Father, the Son and the Holy Spirit since the 'name' used there is singular: and that name which stands for the father, the son and the Holy Spirit is Jesus.

According to Philippians 2:9, there is no name in heaven and on earth which is higher than the name Jesus. The disciples understood this only when the Holy Spirit came upon them. It is written, "When he, the Spirit of truth comes, he will guide you into all truth." (John 16:13-14)

Unfortunately, some Christians don't believe the Holy Spirit baptism, yet they claim that, they understand the word of God, forgetting that, the word of God is spirit and takes only the Spirit of God to understand it. (John 6:63) It is written, "We have not received the spirit of the world, but the

Spirit who is from God, that we may know what God has freely given to us." (1 Corinthians 2:12)

It is difficult for a person without the Spirit of God to understand the word of God. It is written, "The man without the Spirit cannot understand the things that come from the Spirit because they are spiritually discerned." (I Corinthians 2:14)

So therefore, the Holy Spirit enables us to understand the word of God.

(II) The Holy Spirit helps us to pray. Sometimes, our prayers have not been answered just because, we don't pray according to the will of God. The Bible says in 1 John 5:14 that, "If we ask anything according to His will, He hears us".

And the best person who knows the will of God concerning our lives is the Holy Spirit. It is written, "No one knows the thought of God except the Spirit of God." (1 Corinthians 2:11)

Therefore, when we pray in the Spirit (tongues) the Spirit makes intercession for us according to the will of God. It is written, "We do not know what to pray for, but the Spirit himself intercedes for us with groans in accordance with God's will." (Romans 8:26 - 27)

(III) The Holy Spirit helps us to overcome fear. Example, Peter became afraid when he was accused of being a disciple of Jesus Christ: (Luke 22:55 - 60) but when he received the Holy Spirit, he was able to stand before the Jewish highest religious court called the council with the high priest being the Chief Justice. (Acts 5:27 - 29)

For fear of difficulties in life, some children of God who have been made kings and priests (1 peter 2:9, Revelation 1:6) through the precious blood of Jesus Christ, engage themselves in occultism and all kinds of evil activities. For this reason, the Bible says in Revelation 21:8 that, "The cowardly will have his or her part in the lake of fire."

B. IS TONGUE SPEAKING A SIGN OF HOLY SPIRIT BAPTISM

Tongue speaking is evidence showing that the believer has received the Holy Spirit baptism. There is no where in the New Testament where believers did not speak in tongues when the Holy Spirit came upon them. (Acts 2:1 – 4, 19: 5 – 6, 10:44 - 46)

Acts 8:5 – 19 have become points of an argument just because tongues speaking was not mentioned there when the Holy Spirit came upon them. According to Acts 8:5 – 19, there was a man called Simon among the believers who received the Holy Spirit baptism.

This man was a sorcerer. He became a believer and walked with Philip the evangelist. He saw all the miracles and wonders Philip performed, but he never demanded such power.

But when the Holy Spirit baptized them through the laying on of the Apostles' hands, he offered them money saying, "give me this power so that, anyone on whom I lay hands may receive the Holy Spirit."

The question is, what did he see? And what happened when the Apostles laid their hands on them?

In Acts 9:17 – 18, the Bible says that, Saul (Paul) was filled with the Holy Spirit without making mention of tongues speaking.

Does it mean Paul did not speak in tongues when he was filled with the Holy Spirit? Paul said in 1Corinthians 14:18 that, "I speak with tongues more than you all." This statement confirms that Paul spoke in tongues when he was filled with the Holy Spirit.

In Acts 10:44 – 46, the believers spoke in tongues, but when Peter was addressing those of the circumcision (the Christians who believed the doctrine of circumcision) in Acts 11:15, he just said; the Holy Spirit came upon them as upon us at the beginning without mentioning tongues speaking.

The above examples obviously show beyond all reasonable doubt that, the believers in Acts 8:5 – 19 spoke in tongues when the Holy Spirit baptized them.

C. Is tongue speaking for every believer?

Yes, tongue speaking is for every believer. It is written, "And these signs will accompany those who believe: in my name they will speak with new tongues." (Mark 16:17) Every believer who does not speak in tongues has not received the Holy Spirit baptism yet.

Paul asked the disciples: when you believed, did you receive the Holy Spirit? And they answered and said unto him, no. And he laid his hands upon them and the Holy Spirit came upon them and they spoke with tongues. (Acts 19:1, 2,6)

This means that, every believer who does not speak in tongues has not received the Holy Spirit baptism.

D. Can tongues be understood?

Yes and no. There are two kinds of tongues. These are: new tongues (Mark 16:17) and different or divers kinds of tongues. (1corinthians 12:11)

The new tong

The new tongue comes with the Holy Spirit baptism. It shows the arrival and indwelling of the Holy Spirit in the believer.

It is for every believer. Every believer who has received the Holy Spirit baptism has this kind of tongue. It is written, "And these signs shall follow them that believe. In my name they shall speak with new tongues." (Mark 16:17)

The new tongues are given to believers by the Holy Spirit for self-edification. It is written, "He that speaketh in an unknown tongue edified himself". (1 Corinthians 14:4)

No one can understand the new tongues; neither the hearer nor the speaker. It is written, "For he that speaketh in an unknown tongue speaketh not unto men, but unto God. For no man understandeth him; howbeit in the spirit he speaketh mysteries" (1 Corinthians 14:2)

E. The different kinds of tongues

There are nine different kinds of gifts given to believers in Christ. And one of them is the different kinds of tongues. It is written," The manifestation of the Spirit is given to every man to profit without for to one is given by the same Spirit the word of wisdom; to another the word of knowledge by the same spirit, to another faith by the same spirit; to another the gifts of healing by the same spirit to another working of miracles; to another prophecy; to another discerning of spirits; to another divers kinds of tongues; to another interpretation of tongues. (1 Corinthians 12:4-11)

However, any of these gifts is given to a believer by the Holy Spirit after he or she has been baptized with the new tongue. It is written, "He shall baptize you with the Holy Ghost, and with fire." (Matthew 3:11)

The baptism with the Holy Ghost (Holy Spirit) and with the fire, represent the new tongues and the nine gifts of the Holy Spirit respectively.

The divers or different kinds of tongues are one of the mine gifts of the Holy Spirit. This kind of tongues is different from the new tongues. It is in the form of prophecy in a strange language. It is not for every believer. It is written, "To another; divers kinds of tongues.

The divers kinds of tongues are given to believers by the Holy Spirit purposely for the building of the church, the body of Christ. And since it is for the building or edification of the church, it can be understood or interpreted   (1 Corinthians 14:27 - 28)

However, the Bible shows clearly in 1Corinthians 14 that, there was no order of service during Church service. Everybody did what he or she liked.

For this reason, Paul was telling them that, there should be order of service and also whoever leads them in either sermon or prayer or songs must speak in a language that the congregation will understand or if he speaks in tongues, it must be interpreted so that the congregation will understand and benefit from it and not that, he was telling them tongue speaking is not for every believer as some believers claim.

F. Has the work of the Holy Spirit ceased?

The work of the Holy Sprit has not ceased as some Christians do teach. The work of the Holy Spirit is still in progress until the Church is taken to heaven. The Bible says that, "The gifts of the Holy Spirit are for as many as the Lord will call into the Church." (Acts 2:38 - 39)

And since the Lord has not stopped calling people into the Church, the work of the Holy Spirit has also not ceased. When the Church is taken to heaven, prophecy, tongues, knowledge, etc., are not needed there.

CHAPTER 6

A. WHY SHOULD WE PRAY ALWAYS?

Prayer is a communication with God. It is in the form of request, thanksgiving, worship, petition, etc.

Prayer is also a divine weapon to destroy the works of the devil. Prayer is offered in Jesus name in connection with the will of God found in His word. A prayerful Christian is always connected to the Divine power.

The human being is made up of body, soul and spirit. (1Thessalonians 5:23b)

The spirit is the invisible breath of God and the soul is the mind. The soul has a lot of meaning in the Bible. Sometimes, it stands for the will, emotion and the whole being as well.

The body or the flesh, the Holy Spirit, the human spirit and the devil send information to the mind for processing. The mind of the born again Christian who prays always is able to reject information from the flesh and the devil and accept those of the human spirit and the Holy Spirit, thereby making him or her able to walk according to the will of God. Also, he or she is able to stand when temptations and troubles arrive.

But the mind of a born again Christian who does not pray always easily accepts information from the flesh and the devil thereby making him or her carnal and unable to stand temptations and problems.

However, the only way the mind can overcome the information's of the flesh and devil is to be spiritually minded. And a believer can only become spiritually minded by prayer and the word of God.

Note, Satan cannot force any believer to sin. He can force the believer to sin only when he possesses him or her. He possesses with the spirit of fornication, alcohol, gossip, etc. And he cannot possess the believer unless the believer's mind accepts his deception because; the mind controls the whole being.

Whatever the mind accepts, the body manifests it. It is written, "As man thinketh in his heart so he is."

Satan could not force Eve to eat from the forbidden tree, but rather deceived her. (Genesis 3:1-5) When her mind accepted his deception and ate from the forbidden tree, he possessed her and in turn Adam also by sowing the seed of sin in them.

God made human beings in His own image and likeness which simply means, to act morally and function as God. So human beings were not made to sing, but when Adam and Eve's minds accepted the devil's deception and obeyed him, the devil possessed them with the spirit of sin which is also known as the law of sin. (Romans 8:2)

The law of sin which forces every human being to sin (Romans 7:17-23) was infused into Adam and Eve and this spread to all human beings since we are all descendants of them. (Romans 5:12, Genesis 3:20)

However, when a person is born again, he or she is delivered from the law of sin and replaced with the law of life or the spirit of righteousness (Romans 7: 24-25, 8:2-4) to be able to walk in the spirit which is love, kindness, goodness, self-control, joy, peace, long-suffering, faithfulness, gentleness, etc.

But the devil is still in the world seeking to capture the minds of believers'. For it is written, "The devil is roaring about like a lion seeking someone (a believer) to devour." (1 Peter 5:8) For this reason, Jesus said; "Watch and pray so that you may not enter into temptations." (Matthew 26:41)

Furthermore, the devil is able to fulfill his desires in the Church and in the lives of individual believers when they become prayer less. "It is written, "When men slept the enemy came and sowed tares among the good seed." (Matthew 13:24-25) For this reason, be prayerful and pray always.

The Church as whole and individual believers can overcome the devil's deceptive act only by prayer and the word of God through which faith and obedience arrive.

Other reasons why the Church and individual believers must pray always are listed below:

1. For we (all Christians) do not wrestle against flesh and blood (human beings) but against principalities, against powers, against rulers of the darkness of this world, against spiritual hosts (large number of spirit beings of several groups) in the heavenly places. (Ephesians 6:12)

2. And the dragon (the devil) was enraged with the woman (the Church) and he went to make war with the rest of her offspring's (individual believers) who keep the commandments of God and have the testimony of Jesus Christ. (Revelation 12:17)

The devil fights Christians just because we have been delivered from him and he wants us back. The fight begins immediately after the acceptance of Jesus Christ as Lord and Saviour; therefore, pray always.

B. BELIEVER'S HERITAGE

The Bible says that, "If we pray according to the will of God He hears us." (1 John 5:14) This means that, prayer which does not base on the will of God is ineffective. For this reason, some of the will of God concerning our lives has been listed below to be used in prayer.

1. Those who hope in the Lord will renew their strength; they will soar on wings like eagles, will run and not grow weary; walk and not be faint. (Isaiah 40:30)

2. Can a woman forget her sucking child, that she should not have compassion on the son of her womb? Yes, she may forget, yet I will not forget you. (Isaiah 49:15)

3. When you pass through the waters, I will be with you and through the rivers, they will not overflow you; when you walk through the fire, you shall not be burned, neither shall the flame kindle upon you. (Isaiah 43:2)

4. Fear not; for I have with you; not been dismayed; for I am your God; I will strengthen you; I will help you; I will

uphold you with the right hand of my righteousness. Behold, all they that fight against you shall be ashamed and confounded; they shall be nothing and they that strive with you shall perish. (Isaiah 41:10 - 11)

5. No weapon that is formed against you shall prosper; and every tongue that rises against you in judgment you shall condemn. This is the heritage of the servants of the Lord, and their righteousness is of me said the Lord. (Isaiah 54:17)

6. They shall fight against you, but they shall not prevail against you; for I am with you, said the Lord, to deliver you. (Jeremiah 1:19)

7. Blessed is the man that trusts in the Lord and whose hope the Lord is. For he shall be as a tree planted by the waters, and that spreads out its roots by the river, and shall not see when heat comes, but its leaf shall be green; and shall not be careful in the year of drought, neither shall cease from yielding fruit. (Jeremiah 17: 7 – 8)

8. For I know the thought that I think towards you, said the Lord, thoughts of peace and not evil, to give you an expected end. (Jeremiah 29:11)

9. Call me and I will answer you and show you great and wonderful things you don't know. (Jeremiah 33:3)

10. If my people who are called by my name, will humble themselves and pray and seek my face, and turn from their wicked ways; I will hear from heaven and forgive their sins, and I will heal their land. (2 Chronicles 7:14)

11. The eyes of the Lord are upon the righteous, and his ears are open to their prayers. (1 Peter 3:12, Psalm 34:15)

12. The angel of the Lord encamps around those who fear him and delivers them. (Psalm 34:7)

13. Because he has set his love upon me, therefore, I will deliver him; I will set him on high, because he has known my name. He will call upon me and I will answer him; I will be with him in trouble; I will deliver him and honor him. I will satisfy him with long life and show him my salvation. (Psalm 91:14-16)

14. Many are the afflictions of the righteous, but the Lord delivers him out of them all. (Psalm 34:19)

15. The blessing of the Lord makes rich and adds no sorrow with it. (Proverbs 10:22)

16. I will bless those who bless you, and I will curse those who curse you. (Genesis 12:3a)

17. God is not a man, that he should lie; neither the son of man, that he should repent; has he said, and shall not do it? Or has he spoken, and shall he not make it good? (Numbers 23:19, Psalm 89:34)

18. But he was wounded for our transgressions; he was bruised for our iniquities: the chastisement of our peace was upon him and by his stripes we were healed. (Isaiah 53:5, 1 Peter 2:24)

19. Seek first the kingdom of God and his righteousness, and all other things shall be added unto you. (Matthew 6:33)

20. Ask and it will be given to you; seek and you will find; knock and it will be opened to you. (Matthew 7:7)

21. Behold, I give you authority to trample on serpents and over all the powers of the enemy, and nothing shall by any means hurt you. (Luke 10:19).

22. Whatever you bind on earth will be bound in heaven and whatever you loose on earth will be loosed in heaven. (Matthew 18:18)

23. If you ask anything in my name, (Jesus) I will do it. (John 14:14)

24 .God's healing is for his children. (Matthew 15:22 - 26)

25. For we know that, all things work together for good to those who love God; to those who are called according to his purpose. (Romans 8:28)

26. Whoever covers his sins will not prosper, but whoever confesses and forsakes them will have mercy. (Proverbs 28:3, 1 John 1:9)

27. For the weapon of our warfare are not carnal but mighty in God for pulling down strongholds. (2 Corinthians 10:4)

28. For the word of God is living and powerful, and sharper than any two edged sword. (Hebrew 4:12, Ephesians 6:17)

29. For, effective, fervent prayer of a righteous person avails much. (James 5:166)

30. You are of God, little children, and have overcome them, because He who is in you is greater than he who is in the world. (1 John 4:4)

31. For with God, all things are possible (Luke 1:37, Genesis 18:14).

32. For he that touches you touches the apple of the Lord's eye. (Zechariah 2:8b)

CHAPTER 7

A. CONSEQUENCES OF DISPISING OF PARENTS

In fact, most of the problems which do come upon us are due to the despising of parents. Parents are the medium through which everyone enters the world. Therefore, there is a divine established spiritual covenant between parents and children which cannot be despised.

But unfortunately, many people do deny their parents of material needs by reason of not taking care of them. Vengeance is of the Lord. It is not given unto mankind to Judge their parents for being irresponsible. Whoever takes the law into his or her hands is guilty of the law.

Many people do say that, it is not their responsibility to take care of their parents. This ideology is false.

Jesus said unto the Pharisees and the scribes (the lawyers and teachers), "Why do you transgress the commandment of God because of your tradition?

For God commanded, saying, honor your father and your mother; but you say if a man says to his father or mother, "whatever profit you might have received from me is a gift to God and you no longer let him do anything for his father or his mother." (Matthew 15:3-4, Mark 7:10-12)

This statement of Jesus Christ, means that 'Care' is part of the commandment "honor thy father and thy mother." For this reason, whoever disobeys this law and does otherwise brings curses upon him or herself.

Yet many people do insult their parents and even attempt to kill them as well, all in the belief that their parents are witches and wizards.

It may be true, but it is not given to us to dishonor our Parents.

The Bible says that, "We fight against spirits and not human." The only thing God has given to mankind to use against the devil is to put on the armor of God, which is truth, righteousness, faith, the word of God and prayer.

So whoever this and does otherwise by dishonoring his or her parents, brings upon himself curses.

Below is some of what the Bible says:

1. Whoever curses his father or his mother; his lamp will be put out in deep darkness. (Proverb 20:20)

2. Honor your father and mother" which is the first commandment with a promise that it may be well with you and you may live long on earth (Ephesians 6:1-5)

Parents, this does not mean you should offend your children. You must know that, you are just stewards of the children. The owner of the children–God will one day ask you to render an account of the children given to you.

B. CHARITY, A DIVINE PRINCIPLE OF SUCCES.

It is written, "Pure and undefiled religion before God is this; to care for orphans and widows in their troubles, and to keep oneself from being polluted by the world." (James 1:27)

According to the above scripture, charity is an obligation to the Church as whole and individual believers as well. Besides, charity, apart from being an obligation to individual believers and the Church as a whole, it is also a divine key to success.

Mordeccai became blessed because of charity.

Hadassah is also known as Esther lost her parents in Persia, which is now Iran and Mordeccai her cousin (Esther 2:7) took her as his own daughter.

Mordeccai took care of Esther and help her to become the wife of Ahausurus the king of Persia. When Esther became the queen mother of the vast Persia and Mede empire, she introduced Mordeccai to the king (Esther 8:1 - 2) and the king made Mordeccai who was a watchman, second in rank to him in the whole empire.

The Persian Empire was made of 127 provinces (Esther 1:1) stretching from India to Cush or Ethiopia (the whole land of black Africans).

Because of what Mordeccai did for Esther; the orphan, he became second in rank in the whole empire. It is written, "And Mordecai came before the king; for Esther had told what he was unto her.

And the king took off his ring, which he had taken from Haman (the next in rank to the king in the kingdom), and gave it unto Mordecai. And Mordecai became the next to the king." (Esther 8:1-2, 10:3)

Charity is one of the divine principles of success.

Below are some of what the Bible says concerning charity:

1. Blessed is he who considers the poor, the Lord will deliver him in time of trouble. The Lord will preserve him and keep him alive, and he will be blessed on the earth. He will not deliver him to the will of his enemies. The Lord will strengthen him on his bed of illness; He will sustain him on his sickness. (Psalm 41:1 - 3)

2. The generous soul will be made rich, and he who waters will also watered himself. (Proverbs 11:25)

3. He who has pity on the poor lends to the Lord, and he will pay him back what he has given. (Proverbs 19:17)

4. He who has a generous eye will be blessed, for he gives of his bread to the poor. (Proverbs 22:9)

5. He who gives to the poor will not lack, but he who hides his eyes will have many curses. (Proverbs 28:27)

6. A man's gift makes room for him, and brings him before great men. (Proverbs 18:16)

7. And if thou draw out thy soul to the hungry, and satisfy the afflicted soul; then shall thy light rise in obscurity, and thy darkness be as the noonday: and the Lord shall guide thee continually, and satisfy thy Soul in drought, and make fat thy

bones: and thou shall be like a watered garden, and like a spring of water, whose waters fail not. (Isaiah 58:10-11)

CHAPTER 8

A DECEPTION, THE DEVIL;S FINESSE ACT OF ENSLAVEMENT

It is written, "If you abide in My word, you shall know the truth, and the truth shall make you free." (John 8:31-32) Many Christians are enslaved for lack of knowledge of the devil's finesse act of enslavement due to lack of understanding of the word of God.

Satan, the serpent, was once an angel of God. He sinned and when he sinned, he was banished, expelled, and ceased from being an angel of God.

And not only was he expelled from the angels of God, he was also sentenced by God to be suffering an everlasting agony at an appointed time together with the angels who connived with him. (Matthew 25:41)

And he himself knows that he has been sentenced to be suffering an everlasting suffering. It is written, "What have we to do with thee; Jesus, thou son of God? Art thou come hither to torment us before the time?" (Matthew 8:29)

Unfortunately, the devil doesn't want to be suffered together with his angels alone, but rather, he wants to be suffered by all human beings. For this reason, he is working tirelessly in so many ways to draw all human beings after him especially believers in Christ. And the most finesse of all the ways in which he is working tirelessly, is deception.

The devil uses deception to capture the minds of human beings because; the mind controls the whole being. Whatever the mind accepts, the body manifests it.

God created Adam and Eve to enjoy His fellowship forever. He also gave them authority over everything. It is written, "Be fruitful, and multiply, and replenish the earth, and have dominion over the fish of the sea, and over the fowls of the air and over every living thing (both physical and spiritual) that moves upon the earth". (Genesis 1:28)

Nevertheless, God said unto them, "Of every tree of the garden thou mayest freely eat: But of the tree of knowledge of good and evil, thou shall not eat of it: for the day ye thereof, thou shall surely die". (Genesis 2:16-17)

Satan; the serpent, also came and said unto them; God is a liar; Ye shall not surely die: For God doth know that in the day ye eat thereof, then your eyes shall be opened, and ye shall be as gods, knowing good and evil." (Genesis 3:4-5)

However, Adam and Eve, having heard of these sweet words from the devil, disobeyed the commandment of God and ate the fruit of the forbidden tree. And this is the source of our suffering, pain, and death.

Immediately they disobeyed God and ate from the forbidden tree; they lost their position of being the rulers of the earth to Satan. It is written, "Then the devil, taking Him up on a high mountain, showed Him all the kingdoms of the world in a moment of time. And the devil said to Him, "All this authority I will give you, and their glory; for this has been delivered to me." (Luke 4:5-6) Their relationship with God ceased. They became servants and slaves to Satan.

Unfortunately, All human beings became victim of their disobedience and its consequences (Roman 3:23, 5:12) since we are all descendants of Adam and Eve. (Genesis 3:20)

But, since God still loved us and did not want us to be suffered with the devil, (Matthew 25:41) He made a promise to make salvation available to all nations by breaking the enmity between human beings and him through one man. It is written, "All we like sheep have gone astray; we have turned every one to his own way; and the Lord hath laid on him the iniquity of us all. He hath put him to grief: when thou shall make his soul an offering for sin" (Isaiah 53:6-10)

However, the man whom God was to make salvation available to all human beings was promised by God to pass through Abraham and Sarah. It is written, "But my covenant will I establish with Isaac, which Sarah shall bear unto thee." (Genesis 17:21)

And the man, by whom God was to make salvation available to all the families of the earth through the descendants of Abraham and Sarah, was Jesus Christ and nobody else. (Galatians 3:16, Acts 3:25-26)

God sent Jesus Christ to come and die for us (Isaiah 53:3-12) so that whoever believes in Him shall be saved from the eternal punishment. (John 3:16)

However, this same Satan has advanced himself in his deception, in that, he doesn't reveal himself any more as a serpent to deceive human beings but rather, as God, the creator of all things. It is written, "And for no wonder! For Satan himself transforms himself into an angel of light." (2 Corinthians 11:14)

Satan has revealed himself as God to some people; using them to deceive the whole world that, Jesus Christ did not die for our sins; neither is He the only way to Heaven. And the most dangerous aspect of this is that, he backs this deception with the word of God due to our low level of understanding of the word of God.

He said to Jesus, "If thou be the son of God, cast thyself down from hence: For it is written, "He shall give his angels charge over thee, to keep thee, and in their hands they shall bear thee up, lest at any time thou dash thy foot against a stone." (Luke 4:9-10)

The devil quoted this from Psalm 91:11-12 to deceive Jesus; thinking that, Jesus is about without understanding. Any religion or spiritual body that teaches that, Jesus Christ did not die for our sins are of the devil. The only way by which God saves human beings from spiritual death or separation from God that leads to eternal punishment is through Jesus Christ and nobody else. (Acts 4; 12)

Whoever has not accepted Jesus Christ as Lord and savior, is destined to hell irrespective of belonging to a religion. Jesus Christ is God's only power of salvation.

Moreover, this same Satan in his deception has entered into the Church or the body of Christ to anoint some people as his ministers; using them to deceive believers in Christ who have been saved through the precious blood of Jesus Christ with miracles, prophecies, vision, healing, signs, wonders, false doctrines and teachings.

In fact, miracles, prophecies, vision, healing, signs and wonders are associated with the Gospel and they are part of it. Because of this, the devil is also using them through his ministers within the Church to deceive believers in Christ.

Unfortunately, due to lack of understanding of the word of God, many believers in Christ are unable to detect the ministers of the devil within the Church by their words and deeds hence they are taken captive. Believers in Christ, the devil is using deception to draw all human beings after him especially believers in Christ. And we cannot overcome him without the understanding of the word of God.

Jesus Christ himself, being the Lord of lords and King of kings overcame the devil's deception through the word of God. For this reason, believers in Christ, let us give ourselves to the word of God and its understanding through the inspiration of the Holy Spirit because, it is the only way we can overcome the devil's deception.

B. THE END TIME EVENTS

It is written, "When ye therefore shall see the abomination of desolation, spoken of by Daniel the prophet, stand in the holy place, whoso readeth, let him understand." (Matthew 24:15)

When prophecy is fulfilled, it strengthens faith but its ignorance weakens faith.

Many people both Christians and non Christians are surprised and disturbed about the rampant rise of false prophets and other atrocious events within and outside the body of Christ due to their lack of knowledge, that, such events must occur.

As a result of this, some of the Bible prophecies concerning those events have been listed in this book to make people aware that, their occurrences are in fulfillment of prophecies. Interestingly, their occurrences prove the credibility and authenticity of the Bible.

Below are some of the Bible prophecies concerning the events of the end time:

But thou, O Daniel shut the words, and seal the book, even to the time of the end: many shall run to and fro, and knowledge shall be increased. (Daniel 12:4)

But when you hear of wars and commotions, be not terrified; these things must first come to pass but the end is not yet. For nations shall rise against nation and kingdom against kingdom. And great earthquakes shall be in various places, and famine, pestilence; and fearful sight and great signs shall be from heaven. (Luke 21:9 - 11)

I will show wonders in the heavens and on the earth, blood and fire and billows of smoke. The sun will be turned to darkness and moon to blood before the coming of the great day. (Mark 13:24 – 25, Joel 2:30 - 31)

But know this, that in the last days perilous times will come; people will be lovers of themselves, lovers of money, boasters, proud, blasphemers, unholy, unforgiving, unloving, slanderers, without self-control, brutal, despisers of good, traitors, headstrong, haughty, lovers of pleasure rather than lovers of God; having a form of godliness but denying its power. (2 Timothy 3:1 -5)

And many false prophets shall rise and shall deceive many and because iniquity shall abound, the love of many shall grow cold. (Mathew 24:11 - 12)

For the time will come when they will not endure sound doctrine, but after their own lust shall they heap to themselves teachers, having itching ears, and they shall turn away their ears from the truth, and shall be turned to fables. (2 Timothy 4: 3 - 4)

Now, the spirit expressly says that, in the latter times some will depart from the faith, giving heed to deceiving spirits and doctrines of demons, speaking lies in hypocrisy, having their own conscience seared with a hot iron forbidding to marry, and commanding to abstain from meats which God created to be received with thanksgiving by those who believe and know the truth. (1Timothy 4: 1 - 3)

Knowing this first that, scoffers will come in the last days, walking according to their own lust. And saying, where is the promise of his coming? For since the fathers fell asleep, all things continued as they were from the beginning of creation. (2 Peter 3:3 - 4)

False Christs and prophets will arise and show great wonders and signs to deceive if even the elect. (Mathew 24:24)

For this reason do not be surprised by the rampant rise of false Christ and the prophets: and the occurrences of the atrocious events both within and outside the church the body of Christ, but rather, let them strengthen your faith in Christ; for without faith, it is impossible to please God

About the Author

Daniel Nana Kwame Opare is a citizen of the family of God, the body of Christ. He worships with The Apostolic Church –Ghana. He is a philosopher, Bible scholar, an ardent and a prolific writer.

He is divinely ordained to reveal the mysteries in the word of God for revival and transformation of individuals, the church and the world as a whole. His books are highly written for spiritual, physical, mental and material transformations of lives.